I0455423

February 2013

PIPELINE PERMITTING

Interstate and Intrastate Natural Gas Permitting Processes Include Multiple Steps, and Time Frames Vary

GAO

Accountability ★ Integrity ★ Reliability

GAO-13-221

GAO
Accountability * Integrity * Reliability

Highlights

Highlights of GAO-13-221, a report to congressional committees

PIPELINE PERMITTING

Interstate and Intrastate Natural Gas Permitting Processes Include Multiple Steps, and Time Frames Vary

Why GAO Did This Study

Recent growth in domestic natural gas production, particularly due to increased production from shale, is resulting in an increase in the pipelines needed to transport that gas. Constructing natural gas pipelines requires clearing and maintaining rights-of-way, which may disturb habitat and historical and cultural resources. These resources are protected under a variety of federal, state, and local regulations implemented by multiple agencies. The laws, regulations and stakeholders involved in the permitting process depend on where the pipeline is constructed. FERC is the lead federal agency in approving interstate pipelines, coordinating with federal, state, and local agencies, but FERC is not involved in the approval of intrastate pipelines.

In response to the Pipeline Safety, Regulatory Certainty, and Job Creation Act of 2011, GAO determined (1) the processes necessary to acquire permits to construct interstate and intrastate natural gas pipelines, (2) information available on the time frames associated with the natural gas pipeline permitting process, and (3) stakeholder-identified management practices that may improve the permitting process. GAO reviewed relevant laws and regulations and interviewed federal officials, state officials from a nonprobability sample of 11 states, and representatives from natural gas industry associations and public interest groups.

GAO makes no recommendations in this report. The Departments of Agriculture and Defense generally agreed with the findings, and the other agencies had no comments.

View GAO-13-221. For more information, contact Frank Rusco at (202) 512-3841 or ruscof@gao.gov.

What GAO Found

Both the interstate and intrastate natural gas pipeline permitting processes are complex and can involve multiple federal, state, and local agencies, as well as public interest groups and citizens, and include multiple steps. The interstate process involves a voluntary pre-filing phase, an application phase, and a post-authorization phase with multiple steps that stakeholders reported to be consistent among projects because the process is led by the Federal Energy Regulatory Commission (FERC). FERC coordinates with federal, state, and local agencies that have statutory and regulatory authority over various environmental laws and regulations. For example, if a proposed pipeline may affect endangered species, FERC coordinates with the U.S. Fish and Wildlife Service, which reviews the impacts on such species. The intrastate process can also involve multiple stakeholders and steps, but, unlike in the interstate process, GAO found that the stakeholders and steps vary by state. For example, of the 11 states GAO reviewed, 5 have agencies charged with approving the route of natural gas pipelines and require advance approval of the location and route, and the remaining 6 do not. Pipeline companies must also comply with various federal and state environmental laws and regulations; however, in most of the 11 states, no one agency is charged with coordinating the implementation of these laws and regulations as FERC is for the interstate process.

Time frames associated with the interstate and intrastate permitting processes vary because of multiple factors, according to stakeholders. For the interstate process, FERC does not track time frames, citing the limited usefulness of such data. GAO analyzed public records and found that, for those projects that were approved from January 2010 to October 2012, the average time from pre-filing to certification was 558 days; the average time for those projects that began at the application phase was 225 days. For the intrastate process, because processes vary by state, the time frames of those processes may also vary. GAO found little comprehensive data on the intrastate process. According to GAO's discussions with stakeholders, several factors can affect the time frame for the permitting process of a given project, including different types of federal permits or authorizations, delays in the reviews needed by governmental stakeholders, and incomplete applications. For example, state and local permitting and review processes can affect federal decision-making time frames because some federal agencies will not issue their permits until state and local governments have completed their own permitting processes, according to some stakeholders.

Officials from federal and state agencies and representatives from industry and public interest groups told GAO that several management practices could help overcome challenges they associated with an efficient permitting process and obtaining public input: (1) ensure a lead agency is coordinating the efforts of federal, state, and local permitting processes for intrastate pipelines, (2) ensure effective collaboration of the numerous stakeholders involved in the permitting process, (3) provide planning tools to assist companies in routing pipelines and avoiding sensitive environmental resources, (4) offer industry the option to fund contractors or agency staff to expedite the permitting process, and (5) increase the opportunities for public comments.

_____ **United States Government Accountability Office**

Contents

Abbreviations

BLM	Bureau of Land Management
Corps	Army Corps of Engineers
EA	Environmental Assessment
EIS	Environmental Impact Statement
EPA	Environmental Protection Agency
FERC	Federal Energy Regulatory Commission
FWS	Fish and Wildlife Service
IPaC	Information, Planning and Conservation System
NEPA	National Environmental Policy Act
NHPA	National Historic Preservation Act
NMFS	National Marine Fisheries Service
NPDES	National Pollutant Discharge Elimination System
PHMSA	Pipeline and Hazardous Materials Safety Administration

United States Government Accountability Office
Washington, DC 20548

February 15, 2013

The Honorable John D. Rockefeller IV
Chairman
The Honorable John Thune
Ranking Member
Committee on Commerce, Science, and Transportation
United States Senate

The Honorable Fred Upton
Chairman
The Honorable Henry Waxman
Ranking Member
Committee on Energy and Commerce
House of Representatives

The Honorable Bill Shuster
Chairman
The Honorable Nick J. Rahall
Ranking Member
Committee on Transportation and Infrastructure
House of Representatives

In recent years, U.S. natural gas production from unconventional sources, including shale, has increased because of technological advances. According to the Department of Energy's Energy Information Administration, gas production from unconventional sources is projected to rise by 35 percent through 2030. This increase in production has required, and will continue to require, steady additions to the pipeline system for moving natural gas from the production fields to gas consumers. According to a 2011 Department of Energy report, the recent substantial growth in domestic natural gas production from shale has already brought lower natural gas prices, more domestic jobs, and the prospect of enhanced national energy security.[1]

---

[1] Department of Energy, Secretary of Energy Advisory Board, *Shale Gas Production Subcommittee 90-Day Report* (Washington, D.C.: 2011).

However, natural gas production and pipelines also raise concerns about potential environmental and public health effects. Pipelines are typically buried underground. Their construction requires clearing and maintaining rights-of-way, which may result in the loss of habitat for plants and wildlife, disturb nesting birds, and endanger cultural and historic resources. The disturbance may occur on federal, state, tribal, or private lands. Soil disturbance during construction can also increase the risks of erosion and sedimentation if the pipelines are not carefully designed and installed. Further, accidental or routine releases of natural gas may result in contamination of surface water and ground water, including contamination of drinking water supplies. In addition to the pipelines themselves, compressor stations pressurize the natural gas at various points to ensure a continuous and regulated flow to help transport natural gas from one location to another. Compressor stations may emit methane, ethane, benzene, and other gases, which may pollute the air, and the stations may also cause noise pollution.

Under Section 7 of the Natural Gas Act, the Federal Energy Regulatory Commission (FERC) is the federal agency that is charged with evaluating whether the route, as proposed by a company for an interstate natural gas pipeline project (i.e., typically pipelines that cross state boundaries), should be approved. FERC also coordinates with a variety of federal, state, and local agencies—those that are responsible for protecting natural, historic, or cultural resources—in order to complete an environmental review of proposed interstate natural gas pipelines. The number of federal, state, and local stakeholders and regulations that may be involved in the interstate permitting process depends on where the pipeline is being constructed. FERC is not involved in authorizing the construction and operation of intrastate pipelines (i.e., pipelines that operate entirely within one state).

Section 27 of the Pipeline Safety, Regulatory Certainty, and Job Creation Act of 2011 directs GAO to conduct a comprehensive study on the process for obtaining federal and state permits for projects to construct pipeline facilities and report on the results of the study 1 year after the enactment of the act.[2] In response to the mandate, we determined (1) the processes necessary for pipeline companies to acquire permits to construct interstate and intrastate natural gas pipelines; (2) information

---

[2]Pub. L. No. 112-90, §27, 125 Stat. 1904, 1920 (2012).

available on the time frames associated with the natural gas pipeline permitting process; and (3) stakeholder-identified management practices, if any, that may improve the permitting process. For purposes of this report, we consider the permitting process to involve steps companies need to take to obtain a permit, authorization, certificate, or approval from a federal, state, or local entity in order to construct a natural gas pipeline.

To describe the processes pipeline companies need to follow to obtain permits for interstate and intrastate natural gas pipeline construction, we obtained and analyzed relevant laws, regulations, guidance, and other federal and state documents. To collect additional information available on the permitting process as well as factors affecting time frames and stakeholder-identified management practices, we interviewed stakeholders, including federal officials from FERC and federal resource agencies, including the Army Corps of Engineers (Corps),[3] the Departments of Agriculture and of the Interior, and the Environmental Protection Agency (EPA); representatives of industry associations, companies, and public interest organizations; and officials from state agencies from a nonprobability sample of 11 states. These 11 states are California, Colorado, Delaware, Florida, New York, North Dakota, Oklahoma, Pennsylvania, Rhode Island, Texas, and Vermont. We selected these states using several criteria, including the size of a pipeline network and population density. Because it is a nonprobability sample, the information we obtained from these states is not generalizable to all states but provides illustrative information. To identify the information available on the time frames associated with the natural gas pipeline permitting process, we interviewed federal officials and representatives from industry associations and public interest groups, and reviewed public records. A more detailed description of our objectives, scope, and methodology is presented in appendix I.

We conducted this performance audit from May 2012 to February 2013 in accordance with generally accepted government auditing standards. Those standards require that we plan and perform the audit to obtain sufficient, appropriate evidence to provide a reasonable basis for our findings and conclusions based on our audit objectives. We believe that

---

[3]We spoke with Corps regulatory officials in headquarters and five district offices: Baltimore, Fort Worth, Jacksonville, Philadelphia, and Sacramento.

the evidence obtained provides a reasonable basis for our findings and conclusions based on our audit objectives.

Background

This background discusses (1) the distribution network for natural gas pipelines, (2) the key federal environmental laws that may be involved in the permitting process for these pipelines, and (3) the key stakeholders that may be involved in the permitting process.

Distribution Network for Natural Gas Pipelines

Within the nationwide system of roughly 2.6 million miles of interstate and intrastate natural gas pipelines, the following are the main types of pipelines transporting natural gas:

- *Gathering pipelines.* Gas gathering pipelines collect natural gas from production areas. These pipelines typically transport the gas to processing facilities, which in turn refine and send the products to transmission pipelines. The gas gathering pipelines tend to be located in rural areas but can also be located in urban areas. The Department of Transportation's Pipeline and Hazardous Materials Safety Administration (PHMSA)[4] estimates that there are 200,000 miles of gas gathering pipelines in the United States.

- *Transmission pipelines.* Transmission pipelines carry natural gas, sometimes across hundreds of miles, to communities and large-volume users (e.g., factories). These transmission pipelines have compressor stations located periodically along the pipeline to maintain pressure.[5] PHMSA estimates there are more than 400,000 miles of interstate and intrastate transmission pipelines in the United States.

- *Distribution pipelines.* Gas distribution pipelines transport natural gas to residential, commercial, and industrial customers, splitting off from

---

[4]PHMSA is responsible for developing and enforcing regulations for the safe, reliable, and environmentally sound operation of the United States' pipeline transportation system.

[5]A compressor station is a facility that helps the transportation process of natural gas from one location to another. Natural gas, while being transported through a gas pipeline, needs to be constantly pressurized in certain distance intervals. The compressor station compresses the natural gas, thereby providing energy to move the gas through the pipeline. The gas in compressor stations is normally pressurized by special turbines, motors, and engines. Pipeline companies install compressor stations along a pipeline route, typically every 40 to 100 miles.

transmission pipelines. PHMSA estimates that there are roughly 2 million miles of distribution pipelines, most of which are intrastate pipelines, in the United States. These pipelines are considered outside of FERC's jurisdictional responsibilities.

Federal Environmental Laws That May Be Involved in the Pipeline Permitting Process

Several federal environmental laws and agencies may come into play in the permitting process for natural gas pipelines, depending on the proposed route for the pipeline. The principal laws involved include the National Environmental Policy Act, the Clean Water Act, the Endangered Species Act, and the National Historic Preservation Act.[6]

National Environmental Policy Act (NEPA).[7] Under NEPA, federal agencies must assess the effects of major federal actions—those they propose to fund, carry out, or permit—that affect the environment. This requirement applies to interstate pipelines and intrastate pipelines that must have federal authorizations. NEPA has two principal purposes: (1) to ensure that an agency carefully considers detailed information concerning environmental impacts, including reasonable alternatives to the proposed project, and (2) to ensure that this information will be made available to the public. NEPA generally requires federal agencies to prepare analyses showing the extent of a project's environmental impacts. Federal actions in which more than one federal agency is involved entail the designation of a "lead agency" and, in some cases, "cooperating agencies." The lead agency is the federal agency that takes responsibility for preparing NEPA analyses. The lead agency consults with cooperating agencies that have jurisdiction by law or special expertise regarding any environmental impact involved in a proposed project. Under NEPA, the lead agencies—FERC for interstate pipelines—will determine which of the following three types of analyses are needed:

- *Environmental impact statement (EIS).* This type of analysis is required for proposed projects that a federal agency determines will have a significant effect on the environment. In broad terms, the EIS process begins when the lead federal agency publishes a Notice of

---

[6]In addition to the laws described in this section, other laws govern certain aspects of some pipeline construction projects, such as the Clean Air Act, the Migratory Bird Treaty Act, the Safe Drinking Water Act, and the Wilderness Act.

[7]Pub. L. No. 91-190, 83 Stat. 852 (1970), codified as amended at 42 U.S.C. §§ 4321-4347 (2011).

Intent in the *Federal Register*. The Notice of Intent acts as the formal announcement of the project to the public and interested federal, state, tribal, and local agencies. The lead agency is then required to determine the scope of the project. During this scoping process, the lead agency consults with resource agencies—such as the Corps or the Department of the Interior's Fish and Wildlife Service (FWS)—to identify issues and alternatives to be analyzed in the EIS and allocate assignments for assistance in preparing the EIS. The lead agency will also identify other environmental review and consultation requirements under state, tribal, or local laws. Next, the lead agency prepares a draft EIS and solicits comments from the public; incorporates these comments into a final EIS; and issues a Record of Decision. Among other things, the Record of Decision—which is the final step for agencies in the EIS process—identifies (1) the decision made; (2) the alternatives considered during the development of the EIS, including the environmentally preferred alternative; and (3) plans to mitigate environmental impacts.

- *Environmental assessment (EA)*. The lead agency prepares an EA when it is not clear whether a proposed project will have significant environmental impacts. An EA is intended to be a concise analysis that, among other things, briefly provides sufficient evidence and analysis for determining whether to prepare an EIS. If during the development of an EA, the lead agency determines that the proposed project will cause significant environmental impacts, the lead agency will stop producing the EA and, instead, produce an EIS. However, an EA typically results in a finding of no significant impact, and this finding is reported in a document that presents the reasons for the agency's conclusion that no significant environmental impacts will occur when the proposed project is implemented. This finding is typically based on the use of mitigation measures.

- *Categorical exclusion*. The proposed pipeline project is classified as a categorical exclusion if a federal agency determines that the project falls within a category of activities that has already been determined to have no significant environmental impact. Under a categorical exclusion, the agency generally does not need to prepare an EIS or EA.

NEPA regulations require federal agencies to make diligent efforts to involve the public in the preparation and implementation of NEPA documents. Under these regulations, agencies must provide a public comment period for a draft EIS; there is no corresponding requirement for an EA, but agencies may provide a public comment period.

Clean Water Act.[8] Pipeline projects may also be subject to many requirements of the Clean Water Act, one goal of which is to eliminate the addition of pollutants to waters of the United States. Section 404 of the Clean Water Act requires, among other things, that projects involving the discharge of dredged or fill material into waters of the United States must obtain a permit; this permit is typically issued by the Corps. Gas pipelines may involve such discharges when, for example, they are constructed within a riverbed, stream, or wetland. Additionally, pipeline construction may be subject to Section 402 of the Clean Water Act, which prohibits the discharge of pollutants into waters of the United States without a National Pollutant Discharge Elimination System (NPDES) permit. Pipeline construction is also subject to Section 401 of the Clean Water Act, which requires anyone seeking a permit for a project that may affect water quality to seek approval from the relevant state water quality agency.

Endangered Species Act.[9] The Endangered Species Act requires federal agencies to ensure that any action they authorize, fund, or carry out is not likely to jeopardize the continued existence of a species listed as threatened or endangered under the act, or destroy or adversely modify its critical habitat. To fulfill this responsibility, the agencies must, under some circumstances, formally consult with FWS or the Department of Commerce's National Marine Fisheries Service (NMFS) when the actions they authorize may affect listed species or designated critical habitat. Formal consultations generally result in the issuance of biological opinions by FWS or NMFS. The biological opinions contain a detailed discussion of the effects of the action on listed species or critical habitat and FWS's and NMFS's opinions on whether the pipeline company has ensured that its action is not likely to jeopardize the continued existence of the species or adversely modify critical habitat. In cases where a pipeline project as proposed is likely to either jeopardize the species or cause the destruction or adverse modification of its critical habitat, the opinions are to provide a "reasonable and prudent alternative" to avoid jeopardy or adverse modification that FWS or NMFS believes the pipeline company could take in implementing the action.

---

[8]Federal Water Pollution Control Act Amendments of 1972, Pub. L. No. 92-500, 86 Stat. 816 (1972), codified as further amended at 33 U.S.C. §§ 1251-1387, and generally referred to as the Clean Water Act.

[9]Pub. L. 93-205, 87 Stat. 884 (1973), codified at 16 U.S.C. §§ 1531-1544 (2011).

National Historic Preservation Act.[10] Section 106 of the National Historic Preservation Act (NHPA) requires federal agencies to take into account the project's effect on any historic site, building, structure, or other object that is listed on the National Register of Historic Places. The Advisory Council on Historic Preservation oversees implementation of the Section 106 NHPA authority. In general, the advisory council delegates much of its authority under NHPA to state historic preservation offices. These offices identify historic properties and assess and resolve adverse effects on them under NHPA.

Rivers and Harbors Act of 1899.[11] Under Section 10 of the Rivers and Harbors Act of 1899, projects such as pipelines that could affect navigable waters of the United States must receive authorization from the Corps. Specifically, the Corps regulates any work or structures in, over, or under navigable waters or any work that may affect the course, location, or condition of those waters.

Stakeholders That May Be Involved in the Pipeline Permitting Process

A wide range of stakeholders can be involved in the interstate and intrastate natural gas pipeline permitting processes, from federal, state, and local agencies with varying missions and responsibilities, to public interest groups, tribes, and private citizens.

- *Federal siting agency.* In addition to evaluating whether a proposed interstate natural gas pipeline route should be approved, FERC is the lead agency in coordinating NEPA environmental reviews for a project.[12] In 2002, FERC and nine other federal agencies signed an interagency agreement for early coordination of required environmental and historic preservation reviews in an effort to

---

[10]Pub. L. No. 89-665 (1966), codified as amended at 16 U.S.C. §§ 470 to 470x-6.

[11]Pub. L. No. 69-560, 44 Stat. 1010; Pub. L. No. 71-520, 46 Stat. 918.

[12]A lead agency must supervise the preparation of an environmental analysis if more than one federal agency either (1) proposes or is involved in the same action or (2) is involved in a group of actions directly related to each other because of their functional interdependence or geographical proximity. 40 C.F.R. § 1501.5(a).

facilitate the timely development of pipeline projects.[13] FERC approves the construction of interstate pipelines by issuing a certificate of public convenience and necessity, which includes conditions that the pipeline company receive all required federal authorizations before beginning construction, if it has not already done so. FERC does not become involved in the permitting process for intrastate pipelines.

- *Federal resource agencies*. Federal resource agencies are responsible for managing and protecting natural and cultural resources such as wetlands, forests, wildlife, and historic properties. Virtually all applications for pipeline projects require some level of coordination with one or more of the following federal agencies, as well as others, to satisfy requirements for environmental review:

  - *The Advisory Council on Historic Preservation* seeks to promote the preservation, enhancement, and sustainable use of the nation's historic resources. For proposed natural gas pipeline projects, the Advisory Council on Historic Preservation reviews and provides comments on those pipeline projects that may affect properties listed or eligible to be listed on the National Register of Historic Places pursuant to the NHPA.

  - *The Bureau of Indian Affairs* is responsible for, among other things, approving rights of way across lands held in trust for an Indian or Indian tribe. In addition, the Bureau of Indian Affairs must consult and coordinate with any affected tribe.

  - *The Bureau of Land Management (BLM)* is principally responsible for issuing right-of-way permits authorizing natural gas pipelines to

---

[13]Agencies included in the *Interagency Agreement on Early Coordination of Required Environmental and Historic Preservation Reviews Conducted in Conjunction with the Issuance of Authorizations to Construct and Operate Interstate Natural Gas Pipelines Certificated by the Federal Energy Regulatory Commission* are the Departments of the Army, Agriculture, Commerce, Energy, the Interior, and Transportation; the Advisory Council on Historic Preservation; EPA; and the White House Council on Environmental Quality.

cross federal lands.[14] When pipelines cross the lands of another federal agency, such as National Forest System lands, as well as BLM lands, BLM is responsible for issuing an authorization.

- *The Corps* has the authority to issue permits for the discharge of dredged or fill material into waters of the United States under Section 404 of the Clean Water Act. The Corps also has jurisdiction over structures or work in navigable waters of the United States under Section 10 of the Rivers and Harbors Act. If any activity could affect a federal project, such as a levee, dam, or navigation channel, permission from the Corps is required in accordance with Section 14 of the Rivers and Harbors Act of 1899.

- *EPA* is responsible for administering a wide variety of environmental laws. EPA's responsibilities for the pipeline permitting process include commenting on EISs under the Clean Air Act; it also has the authority to participate in the Section 404 permit process.

- *FWS* is generally responsible for implementing the Endangered Species Act, among other laws, for freshwater and terrestrial species that may be affected by a pipeline construction project.

- *The Forest Service* is responsible for managing 193 million acres of National Forest System lands, through which many thousands of miles of natural gas pipelines cross. If a proposed pipeline crosses more than one federal agency's lands, BLM issues a right-of-way permit.[15] In cases where the pipeline only crosses

---

[14]BLM has authority to issue these permits under Section 28 of the Mineral Leasing Act of 1920, as amended, except for lands in the National Park System, lands held in trust for an Indian or Indian tribe, and lands on the Outer Continental Shelf. BLM is also not authorized to issue permits directly for access on National Wildlife Refuges without the approval of FWS.

[15]Issuance of a BLM right-of-way permit on National Forest System lands is subject to the Forest Service's concurrence and inclusion of necessary terms and conditions to ensure the permit is consistent with National Forest System purposes.

National Forest System lands, the Forest Service issues a special-use authorization.[16]

- *NMFS* implements, among other things, the Marine Mammal Protection Act and the Endangered Species Act for most marine species and anadromous fish (i.e., fish that spend portions of their life cycle in both fresh and salt water).

- *State resource agencies.* State-level agencies are generally responsible for managing and protecting a state's natural and cultural resources. State resource agencies, such as state environmental or water quality agencies, as is the case with their federal counterparts, participate in and review assessments of environmental impacts in accordance with their responsibilities under federal or state laws. In some cases, federal agencies have delegated authority to state resource agencies for carrying out federal laws. Additionally, state historic preservation offices advise and consult with federal and other state agencies to identify historic properties and assess and resolve adverse effects to those properties under the NHPA.

- *Tribal governments.* As part of the planning and review process for pipeline projects, federal agencies engage in government-to-government consultation between American Indian Tribes and Alaska Native Corporations. Consultation is a deliberative process that aims to create effective collaboration and informed federal decision making. Tribal consultations can be a factor in the overall pipeline project schedule.

- *Local governments.* Local governments involved in natural gas pipeline projects may include counties or municipalities that are empowered by state law or constitution to carry out provisions to protect the environment or safety of local citizens. This may include requiring soil and erosion plans or zoning laws.

- *Public interest groups.* Public interest groups, such as Earthjustice, Delaware Riverkeeper, and the Pipeline Safety Trust, advocate for a number of issues, including the environment and public safety. They may comment on a proposed pipeline project during, for example, the

---

[16]Most pipelines crossing National Forest System lands are permitted by a BLM-issued right-of-way grant, pursuant to the authority granted to the Secretary of the Interior in Section 28 of the Mineral Leasing Act.

NEPA process or any state processes that include public comment periods.

- *Private citizens.* Private citizens can provide comments and opinions in venues like public hearings. Like public interest groups, private citizens may comment on a proposed pipeline project during, for example, the NEPA process or any state processes that include public comment periods.

The Interstate and Intrastate Pipeline Permitting Processes Can be Complex, with Multiple Stakeholders and Steps

Both the interstate and intrastate pipeline permitting processes are complex in that they can involve multiple federal, state, and local agencies, as well as public interest groups and citizens, and include multiple steps. The interstate permitting process involves three key phases: a voluntary pre-filing phase, an application phase, and a post-authorization phase with multiple steps. According to stakeholders we spoke with, the interstate process is consistent because FERC acts as a lead agency in coordinating multiple stakeholders. The intrastate process can also include multiple stakeholders and steps. However, those stakeholders and steps vary from state to state, and most states do not have a lead agency coordinating the process.

The Interstate Permitting Process Involves Three Phases, and Stakeholders Report It Is Consistent because It Has a Lead Agency

We identified three key phases in the interstate permitting process for natural gas pipelines: pre-filing, application, and post-authorization. During these phases, federal, state, and local agencies, as well as public interest groups and citizens, may play a role in approving or commenting on the application for a permit to construct interstate pipelines. According to some industry representatives we spoke with, the interstate permitting process can be time-consuming, depending on the size and complexity of a proposed project, but it is consistent because FERC, as the lead agency, assists in coordinating with other stakeholders on the NEPA environmental analysis.

Pre-filing Phase

In 2002, FERC established a pre-filing phase to facilitate and expedite the review of natural gas pipeline projects through early coordination with FERC and cooperating agencies (see fig. 1). The intent of this phase is to involve stakeholders sooner so that potential issues can be identified and resolved earlier, thereby taking less time overall. Use of this phase is voluntary, and FERC must approve a company's request for pre-filing. For those projects that are less complex, such as those that do not involve federal lands, endangered species, or crossings of waters of the

United States, applicants may choose not to use the pre-filing phase. According to FERC officials, in 2012, 67 percent of applicants for major interstate pipeline construction projects chose to use this phase.[17] In the pre-filing phase, FERC and the applicant focus on gathering the necessary information for the environmental analysis, which may involve numerous federal, state, and local agencies and is typically the most complex and time-consuming step of the permitting process.

Figure 1: FERC's Typical Steps in the Pre-filing Phase of the Natural Gas Pipeline Permitting Process

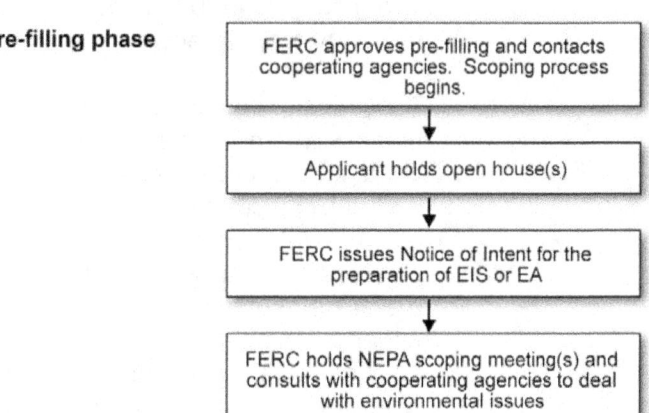

Source: GAO.

Once FERC approves a company's request to use the pre-filing phase for a project, agency staff notify other potential cooperating agencies that FERC has approved the use of the pre-filing phase and hold a planning or information meeting with the applicant and the agencies to discuss land and resource issues and concerns. FERC and the agencies also discuss the agencies' ability to commit to an environmental review schedule. FERC will then work with the applicant and those agencies that are to have a role in the permitting process to initiate the NEPA scoping process—that is, the process of defining and refining the scope of an EIS or EA and the alternatives to be investigated—and begin the environmental analysis.

---

[17]For the purpose of environmental review, a major project is one where FERC has determined that the EIS or EA will be issued for public comment.

Applicants are to hold "open house" meetings in the vicinity of the proposed project to share information about the project with the public. FERC staff often attends these meetings to answer any questions about the FERC permitting process and to invite the public to participate in the process at future dates. According to FERC's website, applicants may incorporate proposed mitigation measures into the project design from comments received during these meetings. After these meetings, FERC will issue a Notice of Intent in the *Federal Register* for the preparation of an EA or EIS and seek additional public comments. FERC staff may also hold public scoping meetings for major projects that require an EIS or EA. Information given by the public during scoping meetings can help the company prepare environmental mitigation measures.

According to industry representatives we spoke with, FERC's pre-filing process was helpful at resolving potential problems earlier in the process, but other stakeholders said the pre-filing process is confusing and may limit public input. For example, one natural gas industry representative noted that the pre-filing phase has made the overall process less complicated. Another stated that it has resolved potential project "derailers," such as issues with routing the pipeline through areas with endangered species, and has saved time for obtaining a permit. In addition, another industry representative said that early identification of stakeholders also increases coverage of potential resource impact issues so that appropriate surveys, mitigation practices, coordination with local and state requirements, and planning for habitat management or conservation can be coordinated with proposed project construction timelines. On the other hand, some state officials and representatives of public interest groups were more skeptical of the pre-filing phase. One representative of an environmental group said the public is unaware of the pre-filing phase and suggested that FERC and other stakeholders specifically reach out to environmental groups during the pre-filing phase if they want to resolve potential issues early in the process. However, another representative from an environmental group commended FERC for establishing an e-mail notification system that enables the public to sign up for e-mails on the progress of a specific project.

Application Phase

Once pre-filing activities are completed or, if the applicant chooses to forgo the pre-filing phase, the applicant submits an application for a certificate of public convenience and necessity to FERC (see fig. 2 for steps in the application phase). FERC issues a Notice of Application, which includes the following: the unique number assigned to the project; the ways in which stakeholders, including the public, can become involved in the proceedings; and the methods for filing comments with

FERC. There are several factors taken into account when FERC establishes a schedule for the environmental review, including the scope and complexity of the project, the requirements of any cooperating agencies, and the requested time frame of the applicant. Schedules may be adjusted if new concerns are identified, new information is introduced, or the number of comments received is greater than anticipated. However, FERC has no authority to enforce that schedule with cooperating agencies.

Figure 2: FERC's Typical Steps in the Application Phase of the Natural Gas Pipeline Permitting Process

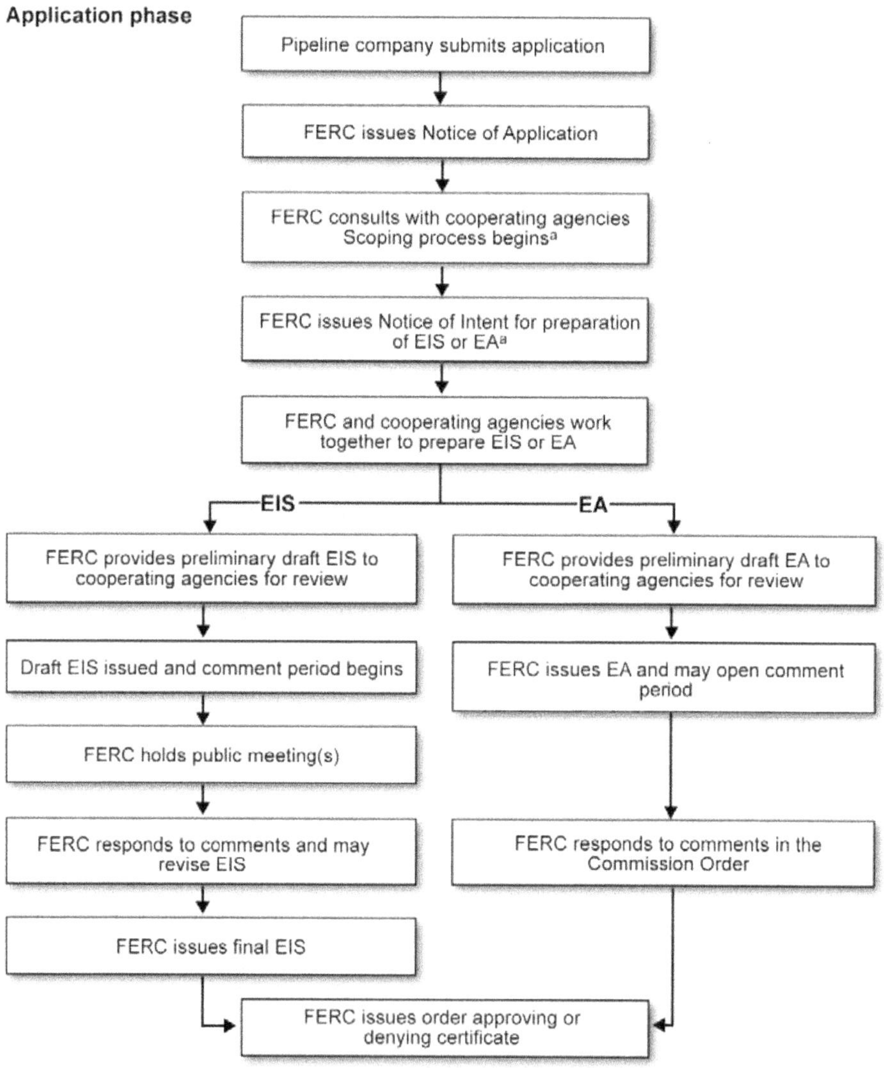

Application phase

Source: GAO.

[a]These steps have already taken place for those natural gas pipeline projects that began the permitting process with the pre-filing phase.

FERC then analyzes the information in the application and begins the scoping process for those proposed projects that did not use the pre-filing phase or continues the scoping process for those proposed projects that did use the pre-filing phase. If a company did not use the pre-filing phase,

FERC will begin the scoping process and consult with cooperating agencies to gather information. Next, FERC will issue a Notice of Intent to prepare either an EA or EIS. FERC, along with any cooperating agencies, will prepare either an EA or a draft EIS, depending on the potential environmental effects of the project. Cooperating agencies are responsible for assisting FERC in the preparation of the EA or EIS for those issues that fall within their jurisdiction. For example, if a project impacts waters of the United States, the Corps is likely to participate in the development of the EA or EIS because it is responsible for the regulation of activities in jurisdictional waters of the United States and would need to evaluate proposed impacts to those waters to inform a permit decision pursuant to its authorities under Section 404 of the Clean Water Act and/or Section 10 of the Rivers and Harbors Act of 1899. The environmental analysis incorporates the necessary information from all federal agencies in one document.

While FERC may issue the certificate of public convenience and necessity before all federal permits, certificates, or authorizations are complete, it will not grant the authority to construct a pipeline without these federal authorizations. Pipeline companies must coordinate with the relevant agencies to ensure that these permits, certifications, and authorizations are completed. This may happen during the application phase or after FERC issues its certificate.

Some states have developed written agreements with federal agencies that establish a process for carrying out their roles in consultation, review, and compliance with one or more federal laws. In some cases, state agencies have received the authority from federal agencies to implement federal laws and regulations. For example, the Clean Air Act gives EPA the authority to limit emissions of air pollutants, such as nitrogen oxides and methane, that result from constructing and operating natural gas compressor stations and pipelines. Such emission limits are established through a preconstruction permit issued by EPA, or, in some cases, by a state or local agency that has received authority from EPA to issue Clean Air Act permits in its jurisdiction. According to EPA, at least 75 percent of preconstruction permits are issued by state and local agencies, and EPA's regional offices issue the remaining preconstruction permits. In areas where the state agency issues the clean air permits under the rules of their state implementation plan, EPA provides minimal oversight because the state is the permitting authority and therefore has primacy over decision making. In addition, state agencies may have delegated authority to process and issue federal Water Quality Certifications, required under Section 401 of the Clean Water Act, and Consistency Concurrences, under the Coastal Zone Management Act.[18]

Environmental permits issued by federal agencies can also vary by state or by region. For example, the Corps issues two types of permits to authorize activities under Section 404 of the Clean Water Act and Section 10 of the Rivers and Harbors Act of 1899: (1) individual permits, and (2) general permits. The type of permit used depends on the type and extent of proposed impacts on aquatic resources and whether a general permit is available to authorize such impacts. The Corps issues individual permits for specific projects that may have more than minimal impacts on aquatic resources, either individually or cumulatively, or are not otherwise authorized by general permits. The Corps issues general permits for activities resulting in no more than minimal adverse effects on the aquatic environment. The following three types of general permits are used for natural gas pipeline construction projects that require the discharge of dredged or fill material into waters of the United States and/or work or structures affecting the course, location, or condition of navigable waters:

- *Nationwide permit.* This type of general permit is intended to streamline and expedite the evaluation and approval process throughout the nation for certain types of activities that have only minimal impacts, both individually and cumulatively, on the aquatic environment. Activities that meet the terms and conditions of this type of permit, such as natural gas pipeline construction projects, are already authorized by the Corps. The Corps district verifies that the project meets the conditions outlined in the applicable nationwide permit. Corps headquarters, rather than one of the 38 district offices, issues these permits. However, one of the Corps' eight division offices may add regional conditions to these permits in order to protect local aquatic ecosystems or to minimize adverse effects on ecologically critical areas or other valuable resources.

- *Regional general permits.* This type of permit authorizes activities that commonly occur in a particular region and that are expected to have a

---

[18]Coastal Zone Management Act of 1972, Pub. L. No. 92-583 (1972), as amended and codified at 16 U.S.C. §§ 1451-1466, § 1456(c) (2010). The act's purpose is to promote comprehensive and coordinated planning for coastal zone development and preservation between states and the federal government. Conservation Law Foundation v. Watt, 560 F.Supp. 561, 574 (D. Mass. 1983).

minimal impact on waters of the United States, but that do not warrant national authorization. Corps district offices issue this type of permit.

- *Programmatic general permits.* This type of general permit is established in those states or localities where there is a similar existing state, local, or other federal agency regulatory program. It is designed to avoid regulatory duplication. These types of permits may allow activities, including work in waters of the United States associated with pipeline projects, to have greater impact on waters than the nationwide general permits, provided there is still no more than minimal adverse effect on the environment. The programmatic general permit will identify those impacts that may be verified by the state or other entity with no review by the Corps, as well as any activities that may require notification to the Corps before verification is provided. Once the programmatic general permit is issued, the state or local agencies review proposed projects to verify that the proposed activities meet the terms and conditions of the permit, coordinating with the Corps' district offices as necessary. Corps district offices receive annual reports from state and local agencies regarding the use of the programmatic general permits. Districts also retain the right to review any proposed project they determine may not meet the terms and conditions of the programmatic general permit.

Most Corps districts primarily use nationwide permits to authorize work in waters of the United States in association with pipeline construction activities. Eight districts have developed regional general permits for certain activities, that may include pipeline construction, and six districts have developed state programmatic general permits. According to a Corps headquarters official, Corps districts may use different permitting mechanisms in different states to evaluate work in waters of the United States in association with pipeline projects. The regulations allow for this flexibility to account for regional differences in the aquatic environment, endangered species, historic sites, state regulations, or other factors. For example:

- In Pennsylvania, Corps district offices will generally rely on the Pennsylvania State Programmatic General Permit-4, under which the Pennsylvania Department of Environmental Protection verifies certain impacts that may occur in waters of the United States from the construction of some pipelines if the project meets certain criteria.[19] According to Corps district officials, the Corps does not use a nationwide permit for these types of impacts because doing so would duplicate a similar state permit.

- Officials in the Corps' Fort Worth district office said they typically use a nationwide permit to authorize work in waters of the United States in association with pipeline construction. Officials said they have not considered the use of a programmatic general permit because there are no similar permitting programs or authorizations required by the state of Texas.

- In Florida, Corps district officials issue both nationwide permits and regional general permits for work in waters of the United States in association with pipeline construction. Headquarters officials said the use of a programmatic general permit has not been considered because state regulatory processes are not similar enough to develop such a permit.

In addition to coordinating with federal agencies on the environmental analysis, FERC may work with state resource agencies and local governments during the permitting of a natural gas pipeline. For example, an interstate natural gas pipeline project that runs through Pennsylvania would require several federal, state, and local permits, licenses, approvals, and certifications, as shown in table 1. However, some state and local actions are preempted—that is, they are superseded or overridden by federal law—because the actions conflict with federal law. For example, state certificates of necessity and convenience, which otherwise may be issued by state public utility commissions or other state agencies, are preempted because FERC's certificate of public convenience and necessity supersedes the state's.

---

[19]The Pennsylvania Department of Environmental Protection verifies certain activities under the Pennsylvania State Programmatic General Permit-4, which are identified as Category 1 and 2 in the permit, while the Corps verifies those activities that fall into Category 3. Applications are sent to the Pennsylvania Department of Environmental Protection, which uses a screening tool to determine a project's category level. Under the Pennsylvania State Programmatic General Permit-4, the Corps will review the project if the impacts to waters of the United States in association with an overall linear project exceed 1 acre of wetlands or 250 linear feet of stream. For purposes of determining whether a Corps review is required, total impacts associated with an overall linear project are determined by adding together impacts to waters of the United States at single and complete crossings that occur at separate and distant locations.

Table 1. Some of the Federal, State, and Local Permits That May Be Required for a Natural Gas Pipeline Project in Pennsylvania

Permit, license, approval, or certification	Administering agency
Federal	
Certificate of Public Convenience and Necessity	FERC
Section 404 General Permit	Corps
Section 7 Threatened and Endangered Species Clearance	FWS
State	
401 Water Quality Certification	Pennsylvania Department of Environmental Protection
Water Obstruction and Encroachment Permits	
National Pollutant Discharge Eliminations System (NPDES)—Hydrostatic Test Water Discharge General Permit (PAG-10) or Individual Permit	
NPDES Individual Permit for Construction Activities	
Concurrence of Exemption from Plan Approval	
Submerged Land License Agreement	
Chapter 110 Water Withdrawal and Use Registration	
Highway Occupancy Permit	Pennsylvania Department of Transportation
Stream Crossings consultation	Pennsylvania Fish and Boat Commission
Clearance (Rare Species)	Pennsylvania Department of Natural Resources
Clearance (Cultural Resources)	Pennsylvania Historical and Museum Commission
Water Allocation Permit	Susquehanna River Basin Commission
Local	
Erosion and Sedimentation Control Plan Review	County Conservation District

Source: FERC.

The process differs slightly depending on whether an EA or EIS is prepared, but in either case, FERC, acting as the lead agency, issues either a draft EIS or EA, and obtains public comments on the environmental analysis that was completed. FERC will respond to those comments, and issue its order either approving or denying the certificate of public convenience and necessity.[20] According to representatives of

---

[20]FERC, or any lead agency, is required to assess and consider comments and respond in one or more of the following ways: (1) modify proposed alternatives, including the proposed action; (2) develop and evaluate alternatives not previously considered; (3) supplement, improve, or modify its analyses; (4) make factual corrections; or (5) explain why the comments do not warrant further response from the lead agency, citing the sources, authorities, or reasons that support the agency's position and, if appropriate, indicate circumstances that would trigger agency reappraisal or further response.

GAO-13-221 Pipeline Permitting

one environmental group we spoke with, the public is not given sufficient time to intervene in the pipeline permitting process and often must hire attorneys to help them raise a motion with the agency because the process is complicated. According to representatives from several interest groups we spoke with, citizens are often unable to take these additional steps. However, FERC officials said that, while the agency establishes a deadline for timely motions to intervene, a motion to intervene can still be considered once the deadline has passed. Officials also said that an entity would be well-advised to file a motion to intervene as soon as possible. State officials we spoke with said that citizens are not well informed of the complicated interstate pipeline permitting process.

Post-authorization Phase

Once FERC has issued a certificate of public convenience and necessity or denied an application, the applicant or the party to the proceeding can request that FERC rehear the case or take FERC to court over the outcome of the case. Otherwise, in order to proceed, the pipeline company must file an implementation plan with FERC including, but not limited to, how the company will implement any environmental mitigation actions identified in the environmental analysis, the number of environmental inspectors the company will assign to the project to ensure that mitigation measures are implemented, and procedures the company will follow if noncompliance occurs. FERC must give written authorization before construction can begin. Following that authorization, the pipeline company must file weekly status reports with FERC documenting inspection and compliance until all construction activities are completed. In addition, FERC is to regularly inspect the construction. Section 7 of the Natural Gas Act grants the right of eminent domain when FERC issues a certificate of public convenience and necessity; the pipeline company therefore has the right to acquire the property for that project by eminent domain if it cannot acquire the necessary land by agreement or if it cannot agree with the landowner on the compensation to be paid for the land.

The Intrastate Permitting Process Varies by State, and Most States We Reviewed Do Not Use a Lead Agency

If a new intrastate natural gas pipeline construction project does not cross a state border, then the responsibility for approval of pipeline routes falls to the individual states, and FERC does not play a role in siting the pipeline. The permitting process for these pipelines varies from state to state and may involve many federal, state, and local stakeholders. Unlike the interstate process, the intrastate process in most of the states we reviewed does not use a lead agency to authorize and coordinate siting and environmental reviews.

| Siting Authority | As is the case with the interstate permitting process, pipeline companies must consider two issues when planning an intrastate natural gas pipeline: land acquisition and the need to identify the siting authority that oversees the location and route for that pipeline. To acquire rights to the land necessary to build the pipeline, pipeline companies will generally attempt to negotiate right-of-way agreements with individual landowners along the intended route. If negotiations fail, the companies may seek to acquire the land through eminent domain proceedings. There is no uniform standard for right-of-way agreements and eminent domain authority, and procedures vary by state. However, BLM will process permits for intrastate natural gas pipelines located on federal lands administered by the Bureau. |

Of the 11 states we reviewed, 5 have agencies charged with siting intrastate natural gas pipelines. These 5 states require advance approval of the location and the route of the pipeline. The remaining 6 do not have siting agencies that require advance approval of location and route. Table 2 shows these differences among the states we examined.

Table 2: Processes of 11 Selected States for Approving the Siting of an Intrastate Natural Gas Pipeline

State	State agency that issues siting permit	Intrastate pipeline siting process
California	None	According to officials from the California Public Utility Commission, once a natural gas pipeline company has received authority from the commission to operate in a certain service territory, it does not need to seek further authority from the commission to construct additional pipelines.
Colorado	None	According to officials at the Colorado Public Utilities Commission, the commission does not require pipeline companies to obtain a siting permit, but it does require them to notify the commission in writing of certain planned intrastate natural gas pipelines no later than 20 days before the anticipated construction.
Delaware	None	According to officials at the Delaware Public Service Commission, the commission does not require pipeline companies to obtain a siting permit, but many companies voluntarily notify the commission before construction. If the pipeline is associated with an extension of a pipeline company's service territory, then a company would need the commission's approval to extend the service territory.
Florida	Florida Department of Environmental Protection	According to officials at the Florida Department of Environmental Protection, the department is the lead agency for siting intrastate natural gas pipelines that meet certain criteria. This department coordinates with other affected state agencies and local governments and issues a final certification that must be approved by the governor, the attorney general, the chief financial officer, and the commissioner of agriculture.

State	State agency that issues siting permit	Intrastate pipeline siting process
New York	New York State Public Service Commission	According to officials at the New York State Department of Public Service, the Public Service Commission is the decision-making body that authorizes the siting and construction of major gas transmission facilities by issuing a Certificate of Environmental Compatibility and Public Need. The applicant must submit its proposed project to the commission, with copies to several state agencies, and each municipality in which any portion of the pipeline is to be located. If the commission issues a certificate, the applicant must submit environmental management and construction plans and other post-certificate filings. Construction begins when final right-of-way acquisitions are completed and all preconstruction conditions of the certificate are met.
North Dakota	North Dakota Public Service Commission	According to officials at the North Dakota Public Service Commission, the commission has authority over the siting of intrastate pipelines. The commission also developed criteria for exclusion and avoidance areas—such as national and state parks, areas critical to the life stages of threatened or endangered species, and historical resources. Pipeline companies must discuss these areas in the application process. These areas may be located within a pipeline corridor, but at no given point can these areas encompass more than 50 percent of the corridor unless there is no reasonable alternative.
Oklahoma	None	According to officials at the Oklahoma Corporation Commission, pipeline siting is a managerial decision on the part of the company; the state does not get involved.
Pennsylvania	None	According to officials from the Pennsylvania Department of Environmental Protection and the Pennsylvania Public Utility Commission, no state agency has siting authority in Pennsylvania.
Rhode Island	Energy Facility Siting Board	According to officials at the Rhode Island Public Utilities Commission, the Energy Facility Siting Board is the authority for all licenses or permits required for the siting, construction, or alteration of a major energy facility in the state, including natural gas pipelines. The pipeline company is responsible for obtaining all permits needed for the siting board, including all permitting and licensing under the purview of the state's Department of Environmental Management, which is outside of the siting board's jurisdiction.
Texas	None	According to officials at the Railroad Commission of Texas, common carrier and gas utility pipeline companies have statutory right of eminent domain and may obtain right-of-way to construct intrastate pipelines without any prior approval or permit.
Vermont	Vermont Public Service Board	According to officials at the Vermont Public Service Department and the Agency of Natural Resources, to construct natural gas pipelines, applicants must obtain a Certificate of Public Good from the Vermont Public Service Board, which collaborates with the department and the Vermont Agency of Natural Resources on a comprehensive land use review. Applicants are also likely to be required to obtain individual environmental permits from the Agency of Natural Resources.

Source: GAO analysis of state documents and interviews with state officials.

As the table shows, the requirements of the application process differ from Florida—which generally requires state certification before constructing certain intrastate natural gas pipelines—to Texas, which does not require pipeline companies to obtain a permit to construct an intrastate pipeline and which gives natural gas utility pipeline companies statutory right of eminent domain without any prior state approval.

According to public interest and industry group representatives we spoke with, the intrastate process for permitting and siting pipelines needs to be more transparent. In many states, it is difficult to determine the process for pipeline siting and whether the state has an agency with siting authority. They also told us that the intrastate process is challenging to navigate without an agency that takes the lead on siting and coordinating the environmental review, as FERC does at the interstate level. Additionally, representatives from two public interest groups we spoke with explained that it is more difficult for the public to comment on proposals for intrastate pipelines because the state processes are not transparent, and the public may not learn about pipelines until after they have been approved. The availability of eminent domain authority can also change how companies deal with land owners and, as a result, can change land owners' perspective on the process as a whole, according to the public interest group representatives.

Environmental Review

Federal agencies become involved in the intrastate natural gas pipeline permitting process if federally protected resources have the potential to be affected by a project. For example, the Corps becomes involved when a proposed pipeline will be constructed in aquatic resources over which it has jurisdiction and FWS becomes involved if the route crosses an area with a plant or habitat on the federal list of threatened or endangered species.

State environmental laws and regulations are applicable to intrastate pipelines. However, in 10 of the 11 states we reviewed, no single entity is responsible for coordinating all of the environmental reviews, including federal and state authorizations, during the intrastate permitting process. For example, in Rhode Island, the Energy Facility Siting Board is the authority for approving the siting and construction of natural gas pipelines; the pipeline company is responsible for obtaining all necessary permits, including all permitting and licensing under the jurisdiction of the state's Department of Environmental Management. Conversely, the New York State Public Service Commission is the lead agency for the siting of intrastate natural gas pipelines. This department coordinates with other affected state agencies and local governments on the permitting process—one stop licensing.

Time Frames for Interstate and Intrastate Pipeline Permitting Processes Vary Because of Multiple Factors

For interstate pipelines, FERC's public record information system contains documents that provide dates associated with the phases of the permitting process; however, FERC does not track the time it takes to complete the process. FERC officials said data on processing time frames is of limited use when planning a project because the variability among projects can make them incomparable. Using the information available on interstate natural gas pipeline projects certified from January 1, 2010, to October 24, 2012, we determined that the average processing time from pre-filing to certification for interstate natural gas pipeline projects was 558 days, and the processing times ranged from 370 to 886 days. These projects varied in size and function and included pipelines, pipeline expansions, compressor stations, and other pipeline facilities. For projects that begin in the application phase, the average processing time from formal filing to certification was 225 days for this period. The processing times for these projects, which tended to be for compressor stations and smaller pipeline expansions, ranged from 63 to 455 days.

For intrastate pipelines, because the permitting process varies by state, the time frames for those processes may also vary. As is the case with interstate pipelines, time frames associated with permitting of intrastate pipelines may also vary because of differences in stakeholders, siting, and environmental factors and range in the amount of time to complete the permitting process. Some state agencies gave us estimates of time frames for specific parts of the process, but we found little comprehensive data on the intrastate permitting process in the states we reviewed. Comprehensive data are probably not available because most states do not have a lead agency that coordinates all the reviews necessary to complete the permitting process. For example, North Dakota state officials estimated that the siting part of the permitting process for intrastate pipelines takes just over 3 months; however, these 3 months do not include the time associated with any federal or state environmental reviews that may be necessary for pipeline projects. A New York state official estimated that the entire intrastate permitting process, including siting and all environmental reviews, takes 60 to 90 days for small pipelines, 3 to 6 months for medium pipelines, and 12 to 18 months for large pipelines. However, according to the official, these time frames vary depending on the complexity of the project and public opposition.

The following factors can further affect the time frame for an interstate or intrastate pipeline project's permitting process, as our stakeholders explained:

- *Corps Section 404 Clean Water Act and Section 10 Rivers and Harbors Act permitting.* The Corps does not have statutory deadlines or time frames for evaluating applications for natural gas pipelines or other types of regulated activities. However, the Corps has two performance measures specific to the timing of permit decisions. For standard individual permits, the Corps has a goal of completing its reviews and making permit decisions for 50 percent of permit applications within 120 days from receiving complete applications. In fiscal year 2011, the Corps reported that it had issued a decision on 71 percent of these applications within 120 days. The Corps has a goal of processing 75 percent of general permits within 60 days from receiving a complete request. In fiscal year 2011, the Corps reported that it had acted on 90 percent of these requests within 60 days. However, a headquarters official explained that the Corps collects information on time frames for reviewing applications and issuing decisions for all utility projects under Section 404 of the Clean Water Act and Section 10 of the Rivers and Harbors Act and does not separate data specific to natural gas pipelines from its reviews of other utility projects.

  According to Corps officials, application review can take longer for a number of reasons, such as the time it takes to receive all necessary information from the applicant and the time it takes for other agencies to complete decisions necessary for the Corps to finalize its review. For example, according to a Corps district official and Pennsylvania state officials, the Pennsylvania Department of Environmental Protection had, in recent years, a backlog of applications that delayed the transfer of applications to the Corps, but that backlog has been cleared. Pennsylvania officials said this backlog had probably occurred because the number of pipeline applications doubled since hydraulic fracturing of Marcellus Shale began in Pennsylvania.[21]

- *FWS and NMFS review under the Endangered Species Act.* Federal reviews required under the Endangered Species Act can also affect time frames for the evaluation of natural gas pipeline projects. These

---

[21]According to EIA, between 2009 and 2011, Pennsylvania's natural gas production more than quadrupled due to expanded horizontal drilling combined with hydraulic fracturing. Hydraulic fracturing involves pumping water, sand, and chemical additives into oil and gas wells at high enough pressure to fracture underground rock formations and allow oil or gas to flow. When combined with horizontal drilling, hydraulic fracturing allows operators to fracture the rock formation along the entire horizontal portion of a well, increasing the number of pathways through which oil or gas can flow.

GAO-13-221 Pipeline Permitting

projects can be permitted under the act in two ways. First, under section 7 of the act, federal agencies must ensure that any action they carry out (or actions of a nonfederal party that require a federal agency's approval, permit, or funding) is unlikely to jeopardize the continued existence of a listed species or destroy or adversely modify its critical habitat.[22] To fulfill this responsibility, federal agencies must consult with either FWS or NMFS (whichever agency has jurisdiction) when their actions may affect listed species or critical habitat. Formal consultations generally result in the issuance by FWS or NMFS of reports known as "biological opinions," which discuss in detail the effects of proposed actions on listed species and their critical habitat, as well as that agency's opinion on whether a proposed action is likely to jeopardize a species' continued existence or destroy or adversely modify its critical habitat. The opinion also determines the quantity or extent of anticipated "incidental take"[23]—that is, take that is not intentional but occurs nonetheless as a result of carrying out an agency action. FERC consults with FWS or NMFS under section 7 of the Endangered Species Act for the construction of interstate natural gas pipelines.

For actions without a federal nexus (i.e., no federal funding, permit, or license), section 10 of the Endangered Species Act provides an avenue for entities to obtain permits for activities—such as the construction of a natural gas pipeline or a highway—that may result in the take of a listed species. An applicant for a permit is to submit a habitat conservation plan that shows the likely impact of the planned action; steps taken to minimize and mitigate the impact; funding for the mitigation; alternatives considered and rejected; and any other measures FWS or NMFS may require. According to representatives of an industry association we spoke with, their members report successful coordination of consultations under section 7 of the act because a federal agency, such as FERC for interstate pipelines and BLM for some intrastate pipelines, can assist the pipeline company in

---

[22]For the purpose of this report, the term "listed species" includes not only the species itself but also its critical habitat, if critical habitat has been designated under the Endangered Species Act.

[23]The Endangered Species Act provides direction for conserving threatened and endangered species. Specifically, section 9 of the act generally prohibits the "take" of endangered species. The act defines take as "to harass, harm, pursue, hunt, shoot, wound, kill, trap, capture, or collect, or to attempt to engage in any such conduct." 16 U.S.C. § 1532(19) (2006).

establishing long-term mitigation plans and other requirements for section 7 approval. The section 10 review process is less preferable, according to representatives, because the pipeline company is responsible for coordinating the relevant federal and state agency reviews and permits before the section 10 review is completed, which takes more time than a section 7 consultation.

- *Delays in state and local government reviews.* State and local permitting and review processes can take time and affect federal decision-making time frames because some federal agencies cannot issue their permits until state and local governments have completed their own permitting processes. For example, permits for federal programs delegated to states, such as section 401 of the Clean Water Act, can take time for state agencies to review and are needed for the Corps to issue an individual permit or verify a general permit. According to a Corps official and state officials, some states experience delays in completing these reviews.

- *Overlap of federal, state, and local environmental processes.* According to representatives of an industry association we spoke with, jurisdictional overlaps between federal, state, and local agencies force pipeline companies to obtain environmental permits or approvals from more than one level of government for the same activity. In some cases, the pipeline company must coordinate the pipeline route with the requirements for permits and reviews required by up to four different authorities at the federal, state, county, and municipal level. For example, these representatives stated, EPA's regional office serving Alabama requires that ordinances be adopted to create a local construction storm water permitting program to regulate the same construction sites that the Alabama Department of Environmental Management already regulates under its statewide program. According to these representatives, natural gas pipeline projects throughout the state of Alabama are required to comply with the state issued general permit as well as overlapping permits for the same activities in any of the 67 counties and hundreds of small towns that their projects may pass through. These industry representatives reported project delays and resource allocation constraints because several layers of reviews and permits involving various federal, state, and local stakeholders often take place to address the same environmental issues for the same natural gas project. However, according to representatives of public interest groups we spoke with, efforts to combine federal, state, and local processes can undermine the opportunity for public comment.

- *Incomplete applications.* Officials in all of the Corps district offices that we spoke with reported that incomplete applications may delay their review because applicants need time to revise their information. Applications are considered incomplete for a variety of reasons. For example, the application may be missing jurisdictional information (i.e., where the waters of the United States are located relative to the project) or the applicant may miscalculate impacts. Officials from a state resource agency told us that environmental consultants, hired and given processing deadlines by pipeline companies, may submit incomplete applications in order to meet those deadlines. According to a Corps headquarters official, if applicants do not submit all of the appropriate documentation, the permit process may be delayed.

- *Project opposition.* Public opposition and litigation can lengthen the time needed to review a pipeline project or even lead to the cancellation of a project. For example, public interest groups can work with the public to request extended comment periods and public hearings for proposed natural gas pipeline projects that may adversely affect the environmental resources in the area.

Natural Gas Pipeline Stakeholders Identified Management Practices to Improve the Permitting Process

According to officials from federal and state agencies and representatives from industry and public interest groups we interviewed, several management practices could be implemented to help overcome some of the challenges of a complex permitting process identified by these stakeholders. These practices would help overcome the challenges involved in implementing an efficient permitting process and obtaining public comments on pipeline projects. In this regard, in March 2012, the president signed Executive Order 13604, which aims to institutionalize best practices and reduce the amount of time required to make permitting and review decisions for infrastructure projects, including pipelines.[24] Stakeholders we spoke with and the administration, in its plan for implementing the executive order, identified the following management practices as effective, among others:

- *Ensuring a lead agency is coordinating the efforts of federal, state, and local permitting processes for intrastate pipelines.* Representatives from industry and public interest groups we

---

[24]Executive Order No. 13604, *Improving Performance of Federal Permitting and Review of Infrastructure Projects* (Mar. 22, 2012).

interviewed noted that the interstate process is better coordinated than intrastate processes because FERC is designated as the lead agency for the environmental review of a pipeline project, but there is no similar lead agency in the intrastate permitting process. Representatives of a public interest group noted that the absence of a lead agency also makes it difficult for the public to become involved in the permitting process because citizens often do not know which agency to contact about a pipeline project.

In that regard, in July 2001, the Interstate Oil and Gas Compact Commission and the National Association of Regulatory Utility Commissioners' pipeline siting working group recommended that each state establish a coordinating effort within the governor's office to monitor and assist in expediting the permitting process, while eliminating duplication of activities among state and local permitting entities. They further recommended that states identify all participants in the permitting process, consider naming a lead agency to monitor processing schedules within existing regulatory requirements, and determine information that needs to be communicated to the public.

- *Ensure effective collaboration of the numerous stakeholders.* Stakeholders we interviewed emphasized the importance of collaboration among the numerous stakeholders involved in the permitting process. Some federal officials noted delays occur in the permitting process when stakeholders do not collaborate effectively. For example, a federal agency's permitting process may be delayed if it receives insufficient information from a cooperating agency. The federal plan for implementation of Executive Order 13604 identified several examples of best practices to enhance interagency coordination. Some federal agencies have memorandums of understanding or agreements with other agencies to establish collaborative relationships that relate to the permitting process. For example, as described earlier, FERC and nine other agencies signed an interagency agreement for early coordination of required environmental and historic preservation reviews to encourage the timely development of pipeline projects. FERC and FWS also have a memorandum of understanding that focuses on avoiding or minimizing adverse impacts on migratory birds and strengthening migratory bird conservation through enhanced collaboration.

- *Providing planning tools to help companies plan routes for pipelines and avoid sensitive environmental resources.* Industry representatives we spoke with noted that there is a need for technology tools that can aid in the proper routing of pipelines when companies are planning a project. Such tools should involve mapping software and best practices for specific areas of the country so that agencies do not need to reassess environmental impacts each time a company plans a project. These tools would also allow the project to be routed with the fewest environmental impacts at an early stage in the pipeline company's design process. Without such tools, it is difficult for pipeline companies to route a project given the various federal, state, and local requirements that are not available in a single location. For example, FWS is currently developing such a tool—the Information, Planning and Conservation (IPaC) System—that is expected to let companies determine whether there are any endangered and threatened species in a potential project area and obtain information about the measures the companies can take to help protect and conserve those species when designing and constructing a project. This system is expected to help companies make better routing decisions early on, eliminating the need to modify project plans later in the permitting process. The federal plan to implement Executive Order 13604 selected IPaC as an example of a best practice to "reduce surprises and help project proponents make better informed design decisions early, when there is more flexibility to make minor modification with minimum disruption of the project goals."

Another planning tool that was mentioned as making the process more efficient by industry representatives was the Pennsylvania Natural Diversity Inventory Environmental Review Tool, which screens proposed projects to identify, avoid, or mitigate impacts on federal or state-identified threatened or endangered species. Industry representatives said this tool has been helpful to determine potential adverse impacts and plan mitigation.

In addition, BLM designates pipeline corridors as part of its land use planning process. According to BLM officials, corridors reduce environmental impacts by allowing projects to share access roads and use previously disturbed areas. They also reduce the need for new data collection and land use plan amendments.

- *Offering industry the option to fund contractors or agency staff to expedite the permitting process.* Industry representatives said that many pipeline companies are willing to fund contractors or agency staff to speed up their application review process, which has slowed because of increasing numbers of energy projects and fewer agency resources. For example, stakeholders cited FERC's practice of allowing applicants to fund a third-party contractor to review applications and assist the agency in preparing NEPA environmental documents. The third-party contractor is selected by and works under the supervision of FERC officials but is paid by the pipeline company. Other federal agencies have similar practices that allow applicants to offer funding assistance during the permitting process. A FWS official said this outside support is essential for agencies given the heavy workload and short time frames associated with pipeline projects. However, not all agencies have Congressional authority to accept funds. For instance, according to Corps officials, the agency cannot accept funds from private entities and can only accept funds from non-Federal public entities under specific circumstances.

- *Increase the opportunities for public comments.* According to representatives of some public interest groups and some state officials we interviewed, the public needs to have more opportunities to comment on a proposed pipeline project during the permitting process. A representative from one group observed that, while the typical NEPA process for public input allows the public to comment throughout the environmental review, FERC only offers a brief period for formal public comments. Representatives of other groups mentioned that, because the pipeline permitting process is complicated, it is difficult for the public to know when and how to comment and that additional information from the applicant, FERC, and states would be helpful. The implementation plan for Executive Order 13604 includes multiple best practice examples to improve outreach and education of the public. For example, the Department of the Interior is developing a web-based clearinghouse for environmental information on energy resource development. This clearinghouse is to provide environmental best practices, methods for conducting environmental assessments to aid in decision making, links to applicable federal and state laws related to energy development, and information on the various impacts of energy development projects.

Agency Comments and Our Evaluation

We provided a draft of this report for review and comment to the Departments of Agriculture, Defense, and the Interior; EPA; and FERC. The Department of Agriculture provided written comments in which they generally agreed with the overall findings of the report. The written comments are presented in appendix II of this report. The Department of Defense generally agreed with the overall findings of the report and provided technical or clarifying comments, which we incorporated as appropriate. The Department of the Interior and FERC provided technical or clarifying comments, which we incorporated as appropriate. EPA indicated that they had no comments on the report.

We are sending copies of this report to the appropriate congressional committees; the Secretaries of Agriculture, Defense, and of the Interior; the Administrator of EPA; the Chairman of FERC; and other interested parties. In addition, the report is available at no charge on the GAO website at http://www.gao.gov.

If you or your staff have any questions about this report, please contact me at (202) 512-3841 or ruscof@gao.gov. Contact points for our Offices of Congressional Relations and Public Affairs may be found on the last page of this report. GAO staff who made key contributions to this report are listed in appendix III.

Frank Rusco
Director
Natural Resources and Environment

Appendix I: Objectives, Scope, and Methodology

Our objectives for this review were to determine (1) the processes necessary for pipeline companies to acquire permits to construct interstate and intrastate natural gas pipelines; (2) information available on the time frames associated with the natural gas pipeline permitting process; and (3) stakeholder-identified management practices, if any, that may improve the permitting process. For purposes of this report, we consider the permitting process to involve steps companies need to take to obtain a permit, authorization, certificate, or approval from a federal, state, or local entity in order to construct a natural gas pipeline.

To understand processes and permits required to construct natural gas pipelines at the federal level, we reviewed relevant federal laws and regulations, as well as agency documentation, such as the interagency agreement between the Federal Energy Regulatory Commission (FERC) and nine other federal agencies regarding their coordination during the review process for the National Environmental Policy Act and efforts to facilitate the development of natural gas pipeline projects.[1] In addition, we reviewed literature on natural gas pipeline permitting issues and previous relevant GAO reports. We interviewed officials with regulatory responsibilities at FERC, the Army Corps of Engineers (Corps), the departments of Agriculture and of the Interior, and the Environmental Protection Agency. We also interviewed a range of other knowledgeable individuals—including representatives of public interest groups, such as the Pipeline Safety Trust and Delaware Riverkeeper Network; and representatives of industry groups, such as the American Gas Association and the American Petroleum Institute—whom we identified as having expertise related to the permitting of natural gas pipelines.

To determine the processes for obtaining permits to construct natural gas pipelines at the state level, we selected a nonprobability sample of states for further review. We developed the following list of criteria to use as a tool for determining which states to include in our review:

- size of pipeline network (miles of pipe);

---

[1] Agencies included in the *Interagency Agreement on Early Coordination of Required Environmental and Historic Preservation Reviews Conducted in Conjunction with the Issuance of Authorizations to Construct and Operate Interstate Natural Gas Pipelines Certificated by the Federal Energy Regulatory Commission* are the departments of the Army; Agriculture; Commerce; Energy; and the Interior; the Advisory Council on Historic Preservation; the Environmental Protection Agency; and the White House Council on Environmental Quality.

- amount of natural gas production (trillion British thermal units);

- amount of natural gas consumption (trillion British thermal units);

- natural gas inflow capacity (Million Cubic Feet per Day);

- natural gas outflow capacity (Million Cubic Feet per Day);

- population density;

- congressional interest; and

- recommendations from federal agency officials and other knowledgeable individuals.

Because we anticipated that states differ in their pipeline permitting processes, it was important to include states that ranked both high and large on the selection criteria, as well as states that ranked are low and small. We selected states by identifying the top five and the bottom five of each selection factor. For example, in considering the size of the pipeline network, we identified the five states with the most miles of pipeline and the five states with the fewest miles of pipeline. We also identified the states that were of congressional interest, recommended by a federal agency, and/or other knowledgeable individuals we spoke with. The states selected in our review are those that were most frequently recommended and/or identified in our ranking process. We selected states that were recommended and/or identified in our ranking process at least four times to be included in our review. Twelve states were above this threshold—California, Colorado, Delaware, Florida, Louisiana, New York, North Dakota, Oklahoma, Pennsylvania, Rhode Island, Texas, and Vermont. Louisiana was later omitted from our review because of limited response from the state. For our selected states, we reviewed relevant documentation and conducted interviews with state agency officials and officials at Corps district offices in California, Florida, Pennsylvania, and Texas. Because our sample was a nonprobability sample, the information we obtained is not generalizable to all states but provides illustrative information.

To identify the information available on the time frames associated with the natural gas pipeline permitting process, we conducted interviews with federal officials, industry associations, and public interest groups. In addition, we reviewed documents contained in FERC's eLibrary, which is a record information system of electronic versions of documents issued

and received by FERC on natural gas pipeline projects. FERC provided
us with information on projects certified from January 1, 2009, to October
24, 2012. Owing to time and resource constraints, we limited our review
to projects certified since January 1, 2010, and used eLibrary to access
documents that contained information on the pre-filling date, traditional
filling date, and certification date of these projects. In addition, we
conducted interviews with FERC officials to determine the completeness
of the documents contained in the system.

We conducted this performance audit from May 2012 to February 2013,
in accordance with generally accepted government auditing standards.
Those standards require that we plan and perform the audit to obtain
sufficient, appropriate evidence to provide a reasonable basis for our
findings and conclusions based on our audit objectives. We believe that
the evidence obtained provides a reasonable basis for our findings and
conclusions based on our audit objectives.

Appendix II: Comments from the Department of Agriculture

| USDA | United States
Department of
Agriculture | Forest
Service | Washington
Office | 1400 Independence Avenue, SW
Washington, DC 20250 |

File Code: 1420
Date: JAN 2 5 2013

Mr. Frank Rusco
Director, Natural Resources and Environment
U. S. Government Accountability Office
441 G. Street, N. W.
Washington, DC 20548

Dear Mr. Rusco:

Thank you for the opportunity to review and provide comment on the draft U. S. Government Accountability Office (GAO) Report on "Pipeline Permitting: Interstate and Intrastate Natural Gas Permitting Processes Include Multiple Steps, and Time Frames Vary" (GAO-13-221). The Forest Service has reviewed the draft report and concurs with its findings. The report makes no recommendations.

As noted in the report, the USDA is one of nine Federal agency signatories to the 2002, Interagency Agreement on Early Coordination of Required Environmental and Historic Preservation Reviews Conducted in Conjunction with the Issuance of Authorizations to Construct and Operate Interstate Natural Gas Pipelines Certificated by the Federal Energy Regulatory Commission. The interagency agreement and Forest Service policy have worked successfully to ensure a consistent approach to authorizing interstate natural gas pipelines. The Forest Service also concurs with the finding that timeframes for processing vary based on numerous factors including the scope and scale of the project proposed and the environmental and historic resources that may be affected.

The Forest Service also concurs that the intrastate permit process is less consistent, primarily due to the variability of state requirements. However, the Forest Service works to collaborate with States in the environmental review process when there is a federal nexus, such as when a Forest Service permit is required. When the pipeline crosses more than one federal agency's land, there is a coordinated federal permit process with the Bureau of Land Management.

The GAO report also notes that agencies should offer industry the opportunity to pay for contract support and or agency staff time. The Forest Service has regulations in place that require industry to cover agency costs to process pipeline requests. The Forest Service frequently utilizes the services of a contractor paid for by industry. The USDA, through the Forest Service, remains committed to an open permitting process, public and stakeholder engagement to support our nation's energy needs.

Thank you for the opportunity to review the draft report. If you have any questions, please contact Thelma Strong, Chief Financial Officer, at 202-205-1321 or tstrong@fs.fed.us.

Sincerely,

THOMAS L. TIDWELL
Chief

    Caring for the Land and Serving People   Printed on Recycled Paper

Appendix III: GAO Contacts and Staff Acknowledgements

GAO Contact	Frank Rusco, (202) 512-3841 or ruscof@gao.gov
Acknowledgments	In addition to the individual named above, key contributors to this report included Karla Springer, Assistant Director; Pedro Almoguera; Cheryl Arvidson; Cindy Gilbert; Griffin Glatt-Dowd; Holly Sasso; Carol Herrnstadt Shulman; Barbara Timmerman; and Jeremy Williams.